Through The Long, Dark Night

Poems on Suffering, Faith, and Hope

M.M. Bylo

All Scripture quotations from the Holy Bible
© NIV: International Bible Society, 1973.

Printed in the United States of America
First edition, December 2023
Second edition, August 2025

Cover design by M.M. Bylo

ISBN (paperback): 979-8-9893483-0-5

www.Mmbylo.com
marissabylo@gmail.com

In honor of chronic illness and pain warriors.

I see you.
I believe you.
We are in this fight together.

Contents

Contents

I stand at the shore, the crisp, turbulent water yanking at my ankles. Lead clouds gather and swirl above me. The wind bites my skin and hair.

The only way out is through this.

With the scraps of courage I have left, I step into the surging water, the tide pulling at my feet and legs, begging to sweep me under and away. I focus on the horizon, where He told me to look. I only need to fix my gaze on Him.

One step at a time, I remind myself.

No more than a few steps in, a wave crashes into me, the spray of water blinding me for a moment. I shake it off and press on, my feet finding the shifting ground once more.

Another wave immediately forms, growing taller before swallowing me whole. My feet lose their grip, forgetting the ground as my body drops to the ocean floor. I emerge from its depths, coughing and gasping for air. I tread the water and longingly glance at the safe shore where I can long for something more beyond the waves but never quite reach it.

I don't belong there.

I place my feet back on the ground once more. I won't quit.

And they don't stop. The waves of life ceaselessly knock against me without remorse. I march on. They throw me to the ground again and again. I get up each time, my gaze never leaving my destination.

Again and again.
We keep moving forward.
Until we learn to walk on water.

Sit A Little While With Me

In my sorrow
     Valley
     Trench
Whatever word we choose
For this place of trial
And suffering

Let me speak freely
Without your judgment
Helpless pity
Or well-meaning advice
Spill the words
Festering in my soul and mind

As I return the same to you
Empathy blooms
Strength abounds
Encouragement heals
Hope is discovered
How it's supposed to be done—

Together.

My Own Gethsemane

Even Jesus had a cup to bear
This is mine
This is mine.

Chronic

You couldn't have my mind anymore
Instead you attack my body
Which, in turn, truly
Made a muddle of my brain
So what, congratulations

Isn't this the game you always play
Kill, steal, destroy, confuse
Your tactics nothing new
I'll take my praise to the grave
What have you accomplished

Stack the odds against me
Deal me loyal affliction
Multiply the burdens
For me to shoulder
I don't carry this alone

One foot in front of the other
With hope that moves me forward
The however to this suffering
No matter what I face
I know how this story ends—

No more death
Mourning or crying
No more pain
Amen
And amen.

MIA

Where it all began—

I'm the forlorn woman
Stranded in that graceless July
Frozen in time
Where I watched my little empire
Implode to pieces

The world moved on without me
How could it not
Another *depressed, anxious* soul
Lost to chronic's abyss
One of the millions missing from everyday life

Society worships the strong
Belittles the plights of the weak and unwell
Forgetting those who disappeared, fell behind
Because it will never matter
Until it inevitably happens to you.

When The Invisible Illness Isn't Such A Secret

I couldn't hide this affliction
Even if I wanted to

No wonder
I want to be alone

My life is an open wound
Anything I do

I'm bleeding out
For all to view.

Left For Dead

They see me
When I'm helping
Applaud my ambition and charm
        I was celebrated
        I was praised
Until I disappeared
Out of necessity
And the crowds thinned
        My weeping's audience
        Are these four empty walls
At least I wasn't alone
God remained
My life preserver
        Keeping me above
        These restless waves
So forgive me
If I hesitate
To open up
I've learned to trust
        No one
        But God
But even that is waning
In the wake
Of this agony.

Sickness-Mandated Quarantine

Pull up a solitary chair
Stare longingly out the window
Watch existence outside these confines
Humans going about everyday life
The world spinning
Without your attendance
But don't consider participation
Exertion only leads to misery

Wallow in your unwilling isolation
Witnessing the people
          Moving, doing, being
          Achieving, living
But you're static, unchangeable
Nothing new
A monotonous, necessary routine
For survival and nothing more

The sun sinks low
The moon takes its place
And like the celestial bodies
Tomorrow you will return.

A Fairytale Retelling

Once upon a time
Normality became a fairytale
Daily wished for
But rarely received—

>>> A smoky bonfire
>>> Laughter floats around me
>>> Chirping birds and frogs
>>> Children's giggles of levity

But where's the pain
The imminent confusion
Of course, it's there
Lurking in the background

At the edge of the woods
The wolf patiently waits
For this part of the tale to end
It knows the routine

What a cruel trick
Because the consequences of living
Of being human banish me
To stare at that ceiling once more

This is my reality—
When the mundane
The life I took for granted
Becomes something of a dream.

What Came First: The Disease Or Depression?

When nothing changes
No matter what you do
Day after day
After day after
Day after day
After day after
Day after day
After day after
Day after day
After day after
Day after day
After day after
Day after day
After day after
Day after day
After day after
Day after day
After day after
Day after day
After day after
Day after day
After day after
Day after day
After day after
Day after day
After day after
Day after day
After day after

Depression isn't the cause
It's the aftermath.

Self-Pity Dressed In Its Finest

When I pray for others
I watch their answered prayers descend
Like long-awaited rain
So sometimes I believe the lie
That blessings are meant for everyone
But me.

Honest Couch Thoughts

Maturity and growth
Is being happy for others
Whose lives are being
Pulled together and rewarded
While yours falls apart slowly.

Caregiver's Burnout

Sometimes even empathy
      Runs dry
      Isn't enough
And I couldn't
Even be mad about it.

Surging Waters

The present thunders in my ears
I rehearse it
Always on the tip of my tongue—
       Disappointment
       Anger
My ruined castle
Built of expectations
Guarded by a deep trench of
       Self-reliance
       And striving
Call it for what it is—
       Pride
       And fear
Why *them* and not *me*
Why *me* and not *them*
You've done it before
Will You show Yourself again

It has become my perspective
This philosophy of perpetual
Defeat and dismay
Simply another doubter
Thrown and tossed
By this restless sea
Of grief, bitterness, and pain

Are faith, hope, and love sufficient
To be my life preserver?

Where Are You Now?

I've seen You in glimpses
Throughout my days
The only reason I'm alive
Is Your tender grace

But the darkness returned
Swept in like a bandit
Snatching gifts You gave me
In its destructive wake

What was the point of these blessings
If I held them a mere moment
Before they were able
To grow and flourish

Now but ashes in my shaking hands
A bitter, overwhelming taste
Gravel stuck in my teeth
Your promises like a tease

Don't be afraid
Well I still fear
Do not be dismayed
I stopped dreaming again

Grief is not only reserved
For the dead
But also the death
Of dreams and good things.

Heart Sick

This is nothing
That a pill could fix
Only a threadbare cloth
For a gaping wound

How many times
Can my hope perish
Before I can no longer
Resurrect it?

How Long, Father?

How much longer
Will this deep night continue

Clutching to Your promises
That anchor these wearied bones
To this forsaken ground
My fingers ache like my soul
With its cracked and bruised faith

I fought my way out of hell
With Your hand in mine
Only to descend into this endless trench
I reek of bitterness, rotting optimism
And misplaced shame

My soul languishes
In this long, dark night
Could You be my light
My steadfast guide
And lead me to brighter days?

To And Fro

Did You forget about me
Just another being
On this spacious expanse of blue and green

You assured both suffering and healing
When does this cease
Now or eternity

How do I represent You
Be Your hands and feet
If I can't leave my bed

How do I preach healing
If I haven't tasted it
Will they label me a fraud

Somedays I question Your good nature
When my reality falls short
Of what You can do

But that is the very place
Where faith takes root.

Misery Loves Company

So I shout into the shadows
Despair reverberating
Through these cavern walls—
     When does this get better?

And in reply
The thick darkness coaxes—
     Nothing ever changes
     Don't you know by now
     You're no stranger to sorrow

I didn't care for its response
Though I felt the words
Deep in my bones
But feelings are fleeting
And breath remains in these lungs

No matter if each day is the same
As the one before it
Where else have I to go
Except forward or down
In the mud with the worms?

Sanctuary

My safe places
Surrendered me
To the waves of life
These havens I trusted
    Not to judge
    Abandon
    Or shame me
Eventually they relented
Questioned my reality
Disappeared
Or labeled me a burden

Here's my fickle faith
I have nowhere else to turn
But to the God who holds
My world in His hands
Will You be my refuge
My fortress from this gale
The peace in the oppression
My rock, my foundation
Could You strengthen
These frail bones
And wearied spirit

Will You accept me as I am
And not turn away?

Father, I'm Tired

Can I sit awhile with You
By Your scarred feet I'm reminded
You have endured pain too

Wearied by the journey, its burdens
Of endless striving and trying
To make something of myself

Addicted to control
Believing I'll resolve this alone
Father, I can't hold on

In Your infinite grace
You don't shame me
But gently instruct—

You were not created
To bear this weight
Let Me carry that for you instead.

Trust Fall

Do you trust Me
The persistent question after all these years
Of course I do
At least that's what I utter
In my ceaseless prayers
Because conversations with You
Keep me anchored here

When I say I trust You
I'm trying to believe
That even in this mess
Of infinite trudging
You're working behind the scenes
Where else can I turn
Everything else is meaningless

Me of little faith
The double-minded one
Crying out once more
Leaning on Your words
Like a lifeline—
Surely You're not done
You can't be done yet.

Thoughts From The Rubble

Finding beauty
In these ashes
The purpose
Despite the pain
Feels poetic
Romanticized
Yet true
Nevertheless
If I don't search
For a hint of good
I'm destined
To only misery
And not even I
Can accept
Such a fate.

The Good & The Trouble

I give You the questions
Left unanswered
They will only drive me
To doubt and madness
Two options lay before me—
       Curse God and die
       Or sit at His feet
Let Him direct
Through the storm and mire
My choice is obvious

I stopped searching
For the *why*
And asked *what now* instead.

The Soul's Anchor

I stare out
Into the abyss before me
This endless black hole
My future uncertain
But You've been present
When many were late
Or never showed their faces

How many more strikes
Can I accept
Before I shatter
Face down in the dirt
But in reassurance
You cradle and comfort
My splintered soul—

I've seen every tear
Take courage
I am Your hope
Have faith in Me.

Through The Long, Dark Night

I've taken steps forward
Then forced to retreat
Most daunting darkness
That I have glimpsed before
The winding path stretches on
My destination obscure at best

But You've been ahead
You've already seen
Where this suffering
And the unknowns lead
You've been there
The way is *through*

I place my trust in You
For it's all I have left.

Trench

Welcome to the valley of the slain
Where dreams came to die
Deferred hope bled us dry
Cut off from living water
We lay crumpled in the dust
A heap of silent despair

Can these bones yet live
Can breath return to fallen bodies
Can our graves be emptied
God only knows and commands—
You of little faith
Prophesy.

Hope's Resurrection

Laid in my tomb
Swaddled in rags
This middle line I straddle
Between the grave and deliverance
A refrain replaying in my mind—
Why weren't You here sooner
But Your voice cuts through
The abysmal disappointment and doubt—

Why are you so afraid
Am I not over all
Through all
And in all
Fear not, Beloved
For My glory
I will wake you
From this eternal sleep.

Mission: Redemption

It started with a fire
Flames sweeping over
Everything I grew and tended
This lush forest birthed
From diligent work
Lay in thick ash
Piled around my calloused feet

Take these seeds
They are all that remains
Entombed in the ground
Water them with tears
And Your promises—
       That hope won'
       Always be deferred
       Forever out of reach
       You're doing something new
       You keep Your word

It doesn't look how I imagined
But Your mission is redemption
Restoring broken, dead things
Even so You can
Resurrect me
And these buried dreams.

From The Ashes

Not all is lost
I console myself—
You can and You will
Rebuild.

Humility: The Pill We Need But Don't Want To Swallow

Here I am, surrendering
Trusting that Your words aren't wishes
But promises You intend to keep
In Your own timing

Choosing humility over pride
For You lead, teach, honor
Sustain the humble
Through the depths of life

The meek encounter You
From their weakened knees
You lift their heads
To behold everything they need

Kneeling in the rubble of the life
I built without Your permission
Believing You'll start a good thing
And **bring it to completion.**

No Eye Has Seen, No Ear Has Heard

Too many good gifts
Disappeared
So suddenly
The grief of loss
Stealing years away
But maybe
      Most likely
      Surely
God had something
Better in mind
Able to bring about good
Even from harm.

Promised Land

I can't see past these giants
Gatekeeping Your promises
Defying access

They curse and shout—
Hope less, doubt more
Why do I cower in their shadows

But nothing surprises You
You're all-knowing
From commencement to conclusion

I remember tales of old
A sling, a stone, and faith
Is all it took

You are the giant killer
If You did it once
You can do it again.

Courage, My Heart

I can either wallow or rise
To meet these flaming arrows
Coming for me on every side
Surrender or fight, my sole options

I will not be devoured
I will not bow
Face to the ground
Where despair dwells

Life made a warrior out of me
I won't go down without a fight.

Warriors' Barracks

This battle, this treacherous hill
You've given me
To climb and conquer
Seems unfair sometimes

But of all I've seen and heard—
Comfortable people
Don't find themselves
At the feet of Jesus.

Fierce

Joy is a blessing
I've fought to keep
A daily choice of contentment
Over circumstance's low blows

If you're looking to steal
What little I have left
You'll have to pry it
From my marred, bleeding hands.

Defiance Part II

Lifting my hands to You
A rebellion of sorts
According to my disease
A symptom trigger
My own sacrifice of praise

Somewhere along the way
His mercy became louder
Than my suffering
No one can take my hallelujah
My joy is mine to make

The devil expected my defeat
So I stood up instead.

Deliverance

Where else can I go
I'm asking for the impossible
For the day to stay still
For You to listen to a human being

The night is endless
The battle ferocious
They come at me
From every side

Grant me inhuman strength
To keep fighting
Until You give the enemy
Over to me

I've arrived at the end of myself
Self-reliance and grit
My stubborn pride
Was never sufficient

My infant faith
Needing sustenance
Something supernatural
Can I have some of Yours, Lord?

Death's Shadow

The shadows stretch
Disfigured and menacing
Eager to consume
Any hint of goodness
Or vibrant life
But I've learned
Though they'll be present
As long as I draw breath
They will never overcome me
Until my time here
Is finished.

Just Like Tea Leaves

The longer I steep
In the rough waters of life
The stronger I'll be.

Storm Shelter

This restless tempest
Knocked me from my course
So I settle down beside You
Drying off from the storm

I dream with You
Of sunnier days and azure skies
Flying unabated
Toward new horizons

Someday to soar as the eagle
But until that time
Safe and sound
In the shadow of Your wings.

Not Consumed

The sun speaks
Of Your faithfulness
That even though darkness falls
Your mercies will rise again.

Come Forth As Gold

Be still, oh my soul
God carried you through
The stretching trench
This narrow, demanding valley
The years spent
Took their toll
He allowed their lessons
And my brittle bones
Found miraculous strength
In the wake of heaviness

Be still, oh my soul
I will praise Him yet.

Spring's Eulogy

Lament what could have been
Then hold its funeral
Bury it within the mud and soil
That dream isn't going with you

But take courage
There is more life to live
New dreams to unveil
But first you must plant its seed.

Hope's Refrain

I will not always feel this way
I will not always feel this way
I will not feel this way forever

Maybe not today but tomorrow
Maybe not today but tomorrow
Maybe not today but there's tomorrow

In the waiting I will stay alive
In the waiting I will stay alive
In the waiting I am alive.

Repeat Until You Believe

Pain is not my personality
Suffering will not last forever
Illness isn't my identity
Trauma is not my legacy
Self-reliance is not my savior
My purpose exceeds any circumstance

This won't be the end
Of you or me.

Sufficient Grace

This unmerited mercy given
When I have no more strength within me
When nothing changes
It steadies my feet for one more step
Another day of *not yet*

My weakness and humanity
A better stage for His Strength and glory
I will survive this
And You'll redeem the lost time
A miracle indeed.

Practical Gratitude

Some days I limp
Others, a mere crawl

Yet slow growth is progress
Why do we obsess over this

I'm thankful for the forward movement
And the days I stay still

I'm grateful to be alive
At all.

Little Sparrow

You lost your song and voice
Forgot your purpose
Amongst life's briars
As if everything depended
On your striving
Give up the self-reliance
It's time to sing
To live
And soar above it all.

Looking Up

Hope looks good on you
It brightens your once wearied face
The ache lingers
But the expectation
For eventual good
Runs deeper still
When God is the foundation
Even sickness and pain
Can't take hope away.

Super Bloom

This season is a garden
Not your tomb
Nor burial ground

This is not your end
Even as the bloom
Still slumbers

Just you
Wait
And see.

Until Dawn

Someday dawn will emerge
       Fortunes restored
       Your joy returned
Reaped from your tears
You'll dance without fear

One day you'll hold victory
Taste the sweet blessing you sought
Until that appointed time
Won't you join me here
For a little while longer?

In Due Time

God left nothing undone
His promises always *yes*
And *Amen*
Every detail written
With your good and His glory
In mind
Your tears gathered in bottles
Over the years
Pouring out like waves
Of mercy and grace
Taste and see
With your very own eyes
The goodness of the Lord.

It's All Fun And Games Until Someone Gets Hurt

Running around with my plastic crown
And wooden magic wand
Willing this and that
Whatever I want
As long as I work hard enough

But when life didn't go my way
I chose You to blame
The nerve of a human
Wielding pride
As if it could save me

I treated You like an option
And all You ever did was love me
I have a different game in mind now—
Let's build something new
Just You and me.

Statement

Even if healing stays beyond reach
This dream never materializes—
        Printed in pretty letters resting on shelves
My name soon forgotten

I discovered who matters
I simply want You
Seeking Your face
Not Your hands

You're not a miracle machine
Catering to my will
You are God
The object of my affection

No matter the circumstance
They will know Your name
From my own lips—
I will be brave.

Looking For Miracles

You saved my soul
And that alone is enough
Each breath is supernatural
On its own
And while I can't deny
This present suffering
Ebbing and flowing
Through my days
I won't forget the One
Who redeemed me
From the pit
And gave me
A new heart
Free and beating.

Not My Will

Suspended somewhere between—
        Career and family
        Purpose and calling
        The world's expectations
        My own longings
        And humanities' propensity
        To be anywhere but present
Threatens the contentment
I've nurtured

Not yet
The words tethered
To every heartbeat
And the ever-honest reality
Whispers in the quiet—
        Maybe not ever
A test of commitment
Will it hold up
Through life's disappointment

Yet whatever plan is fulfilled
To that I will be satisfied.

Take Courage

My faith is forged in this fray
The cutting wind and blinding rain
Relentlessly beating me
The waves may not waver
But I'll walk on the water
If I can keep my gaze
Fixed on Him
Build the perseverance
        Unwavering character
        And steadfast hope
I'll need to outlast
This tempest
And any storm near
Or far ahead.

Defying Physics

The waves crash against me
But I have nothing to fear—
        My Savior walks on water
        And He's a patient teacher.

Immovable Faith

Sometimes Jesus calms the storm
But sometimes He calms us
Draws our attention to Him
Beckons us forward
So we can walk on the waters
And when we notice
The waves of life
And our feet slowly sink
He calls us by name
Takes hold of our outstretched hand
And walks beside us
The storm never ceased
But He kept us afloat
        And that's the kind of faith
        I'm searching for.

Ask, Seek, Knock

I'll declare Your truths
Until I see
Your promises fulfilled
What's so wrong
With believing
For the impossible
If my joy and hope
Are rooted, anchored
In the God who formed
And saved me
My devotion fostered
By His character
Not the tangible blessings
I seek His face
Not His hands
What He can do for me

And even if I don't see it
In this lifetime
You'll find me praising
      Asking
      Seeking
      Knocking
Until I arrive
At Heaven's gates
And into the arms of
My Savior and King.

The Sustainer

I'm not looking for a theology debate
Or a character analysis of God
Because I will claim despite denial—
>God has never left me nor you
>Not then
>And not now.

"I remember my affliction and my wandering,
   the bitterness and the gall.
I well remember them,
   and my soul is downcast within me.
Yet this I call to mind
   and therefore I have hope:
Because of the LORD's great love we are not consumed,
   for his compassions never fail.
They are new every morning;
   great is your faithfulness.
I say to myself, "The LORD is my portion;
   therefore I will wait for him."

Lamentations 3:19-24 NIV

References

Chronic: Revelation 21:4

Surging Waters: James 1:6-8

How Long, Father?: Psalms 6

The Good & The Trouble: Job 2:9-10

Trust Fall: Ecclesiastes 2:11

Trench: Ezekiel 37:1-14

Hope's Resurrection: Ephesians 4:4-6

Mission: Redemption: Isaiah 43:18-19

Humility…: Psalms 147:6, Philippians 1:6

No Eye Has Seen…: 1st Corinthians 2:9, Isaiah 64:4

Courage, My Heart: Ephesians 6:16

Defiance Pt II: Hebrews 13:15

Deliverance: Joshua 10:12-14

Death's Shadow: Psalms 23:4

Storm Shelter: Psalms 17:8

Come Forth As Gold: Job 23:10, Psalms 42:11

Sufficient Grace: 2nd Corinthians 12:8-10

In Due Time: Psalms 56:8-9, Psalms 34:8

Not My Will: Philippians 4:11-13

Ask, Seek, Knock: Matthew 7:8

The Sustainer: Deuteronomy 31:6

Also by M.M. Bylo

Poetry

The Silent Advocate

Surviving The In-Between

Not Of This

Novels

University

M.M. Bylo is an author residing in the Midwest with her husband and their rescue cat Luna. Professionally speaking, she has written poetry, short stories, and novellas since the age of ten and minored in Creative Writing in college. In reality, all she dreams about is using her love of storytelling and her own experiences to share the love of Christ and encourage others. You can find her snuggled in blankets and fuzzy socks with a book or video game, wandering the outdoors, or trying to convince her perfectionist brain that rest is productive.

www.ingramcontent.com/pod-product-compliance
Lightning Source LLC
Chambersburg PA
CBHW060351050426
42449CB00011B/2928